JOURNEYS

A COLLECTION OF INSPIRATIONAL PHOTOGRAPHS
AND THE STORIES BEHIND THEM

PHOTOGRAPHY AND WORDS
JULIAN BOUND

ABOUT THE AUTHOR

Born in the UK, Julian Bound is a documentary photographer, film maker and author. Featured on the BBC news, National Geographic and in the international press, his work focuses on the social documentary of world culture, religion and traditions, spending time studying meditation with the Buddhist monks of Tibet and northern Thailand and with spiritual teachers of India's Himalaya region.

His photography work includes documenting the soldiers of Myanmar's Karen National Liberation Army, the Arab Spring of 2011, Cairo, Egypt, and the Thailand political uprisings of 2009 and 2014 in Bangkok.

With portraiture of His Holiness the 14th Dalai Lama, Julian has photographed the Tibetan refugee camps of Nepal and India. His other projects include the road working gypsies of India, the Dharavi slums of Mumbai, the rail track slums of Jakarta and the sulphur miners at work in the active volcanoes of eastern Java, Indonesia.

Present for the Nepal earthquakes of 2015, he documented the disaster whilst working as an emergency deployment photographer for various NGO and international embassies in conjunction with the United Nations.

Photography website: www.behance.net/julian_bound
Amazon Author's Page: www.amazon.com/-/e/B0054G0UKK
INSTAGRAM: julian_bound

JOURNEYS

Women of the Indonesian army, Malang, East Java, Indonesia

With photographs taken from the countries of Nepal, Tibet, India, Myanmar, Bhutan, Thailand, Indonesia, Cambodia and UK 'Journeys' is a collection of favourite images taken over the period of eleven years.

Using both documentary and creative style, the writing accompanying each photograph is aimed to give the viewer an insight into the place and situation in which the shot was taken.

Seeing each individual image as a its own unique canvas, photography can be likened to hunting; hunting to find that one photograph where light, composition and subject all line up together, merging as one to produce a frozen moment in time forever.

And so the hunt continues. Hunting to find that image which captures the honesty and beauty of what lays before my camera lens.

As the occasion rises when all converges to seize those elements of light, composition and subject needed, the hunt for another such image continues once more for another, and another, and another...

Julian Bound
Kathmandu, Nepal

Location: Kathmandu, Nepal.   **Date:** 7th October 2015

Woman sitting in her small café on the backstreets of Kathmandu.

On the backstreets leading from the tourist area of Thamel towards Durbar square, small shops and cafés line the narrow lanes and alleyways that lend to Kathmandu's mystical character.

Location: Lamichhane Village, Sindhupalchowk, Nepal.   **Date:** 21st April 2016

Woman of Lamichhane village.

Sitting amongst her family, the woman never stopped smiling. Pleased that her family received attention and aid for their plight.

Location: Bhaktapur, Nepal.   **Date:** 11th May 2015

Grandmother and grandchild on the earthquake damaged streets of Bhaktapur.

Located 30km east of Kathmandu, the town plays host to Buddhist and Hindu temples and is a popular tourist spot for those visiting Kathmandu, Nepal.

The earthquake of 25th April 2015 caused major damage to the homes and temples of Bhaktapur. This photograph was taken the day before Nepal's second devastating earthquake of 12th May 2015.

Location: Punakha Fortress, Paro, Bhutan.   **Date:** 26th October 2014

Two Bhutanese Buddhist monks enter the doorway leading to a wooden bridge linking Punakha Fortress Monastery with the outside world.

Seeing the monks in the distance as they approached the doorway, a run was needed to capture the scene as together they stepped forward with synchronised footsteps.

Location: Thimphu, Bhutan.   **Date:** 24th October 2014

Before the Memorial Stupa of Thimphu, Bhutan, a Buddhist monk gives prayer between the several thousands of prostrations he has vowed to make.

With numerous shots taken of his prostration positions, the monk remained unaware of the presence of another as he continued his commitment.

Location: Shropshire, England, UK.   **Date:** 18th November 2013

A lone tree stands amid marshland as an approaching electrical storm travels across the autumnal blue skies of Shropshire, England.

Taking several photographs to capture the sunbeams touching the surrounding marsh and bracken, the tree stood 200 meters from the roadside. Within minutes of trekking back to road the heavens opened.

Location: Potala Palace, Lhasa, Tibet. **Date:** 25th November 2014

A Tibetan woman in traditional headdress walks the walls of Potala Palace, Lhasa, Tibet. In one hand she carries a ceremonial spoon, in the other a bag of wax pellets so she may replenish Potala's temple candles as an act of devotion.

Caught by surprise before a backdrop of endless blue sky, her innocence shone through in the blushes of having her photo taken.

Location: Wat Mahathat, Ayutthaya, Thailand.　　　　**Date:** 9th June 2014

In the temple of Wat Mahathat, Ayutthaya, Thailand, a large stone Buddha head sits encased in a tree. Its roots are said to have grown around the sculpture during a time when the temple lay abandoned and overgrown for over 500 years.

Buddha's teachings of patience became a real test on waiting for a clear view amongst teems of photographing tourists from around the globe.

Location: Gyuto Tantric Monastery, Dharamshala, India.   **Date:** 2nd February 2016

Within Gyuto Tantric Monastery of Dharamshala, India, Buddhist monks hold a three day puja (prayer ceremony) for world peace.

Invited by the monks to document the puja, the temple walls vibrated as deep tantric chanting of 350 monks filled the room.

Location: Durbar Square, Kathmandu, Nepal.   **Date:** 2nd October 2014

On the outer edges of Durbar square, Kathmandu, a young flower seller makes flower garlands for ceremonial use.

Just one of many garland makers seated around the square, the young woman's pensive stare and relaxed pose brought to stand out amongst her contemporaries

Location: Rinpung Monastery School Paro, Bhutan.   **Date:** 25th October 2014

In the courtyard of Paro's Rinpung monastery school, novice Buddhist monks break from their classes as dusk approaches.

Enjoying their time away from the classroom, the monks laughter rang across the open spaces of Rinpung's stone floored court.

Location: Drepung Monastery, Lhasa, Tibet.　　　　**Date:** 26th November 2016

✳ Two elder Tibetan Buddhist monks talk together under the endless blue skies of Tibet at the entrance to the Drepung monastic university which was founded in 1416 and located west of Lhasa.

With good humour the monks allowed some photography within the monastery walls as they took advantage of the warm sunlight as winter began its advance on Tibet.

Location: Palcho Monastery, Gyantse, Tibet.   **Date:** 25th November 2014

Preparing herself for prayer, an elderly Tibetan lady stands at the entrance of Palcho monastery in the heart of Gyantse, Tibet.

With photography forbidden within Palcho's temple, seeing the woman standing in sun-rays of midday, the image was taken from the hip, with only the sound of the shutter betraying that any photograph had been taken.

Location: Barkhor Square, Lhasa, Tibet.   **Date:** 27th November 2014

Outside the Jokhang temple of Barkhor Square, Lhasa, Tibet, a Tibetan woman wraps herself up in traditional robes to ward off the biting chill of Lhasa's late autumn chill.

Once again taken from the hip, the woman stood at the entrance of Jokhang after a session of prostrations on the cold granite stone of Barkhor square.

Location: Shwedagon Pagoda, Yangon, Myanmar.   **Date:** 20th January 2015

A Buddhist nun sits on the steps of one of the many pagoda and stupa of the temple complex of Shwedagon, Yangon, Myanmar.

Rich evening sunlight found throughout Asia highlighted the gild golden spires of the pagoda. Unaware of the nun sitting on the steps when the photo was taken, it was a surprise to see her when looking at the photograph days later.

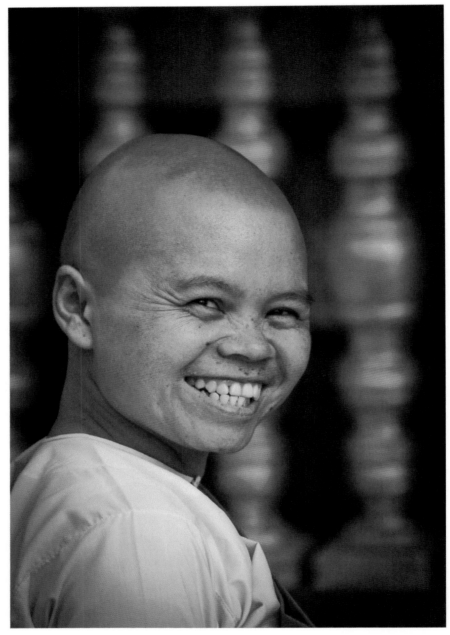

Location: Shwedagon Pagoda, Yangon, Myanmar. **Date:** 20th January 2015

A Buddhist nun smiles within the Shwedagon temple complex of Yangon, Myanmar.

Noticing the camera raise the nun gave a broad smile. This would be the second time her image was captured, it was the same nun who had been sitting on the pagoda steps in the previous photograph.

Location: Shwedagon Pagoda, Yangon, Myanmar.   **Date:** 20th January 2015

Two elderly monks walk the sweeping plaza of the Shwedagon temple complex.

Taken in the closing moments of sunlight, swiftly raising the camera, the one monk held great amusement on having his photograph taken.

Location: Siem Reap, Cambodia   **Date:** 16th February 2015

A Cambodian woman sits with her array of sausages and fish in Siem Reap, Cambodia.

In the market places of Siem Reap, the market traders were not the most inviting to have their photo taken and this shot was captured on walking past the sausage lady.

24

Location: Wat Thmei, Siem Reap, Cambodia.   **Date:** 16th February 2015

A novice Buddhist monk stands in the doorway of his temple of Wat Thmei, on the outskirts of Siem Reap.

With all camera batteries depleted from a day of shooting, this photograph was taken with a mobile phone in the last moments of daylight hours.

Location: Mahabodhi Temple, Bodh Gaya, India.   **Date:** 20th December 2014

An elderly Tibetan Buddhist monk reads scriptures beneath the Bodhi Tree.

Dozens of Buddhist devotees could be found sheltering beneath the tree in India's harsh afternoon sun, all in quiet introspection.

Location: Durbar Square, Kathmandu, Nepal.   **Date:** 22nd October 2015

One of the Kumari of Kathmandu's districts of Durbar, Patan and Baktahpur, makes their bi-annual visit to the outside world during the festival of Dashain.

With strictly no photos allowed, a soldier approached on seeing my camera. He then insisted on my taking a portrait of Nepal's living goddess.

Location: Phewa Lake, Pokhara, Nepal.   **Date:** 12th October 2014

A dusk lit view of Phewa Lake and a lone boat upon its waters.

In the tail end of monsoon season, storm clouds still lingered over the Annapurna range of the Himalayas.

Location: The Golden Temple, Amritsar, Punjab, India.   **Date:** 6th January 2015

A Sikh guard protects the Golden temple with his big spear.

Although fierce in appearance, the temple guards could not have been more inviting for their photo to be taken.

Location: The Golden Temple, Amritsar, Punjab, India.   **Date:** 6th January 2015

A Sikh devotee bathes in the holy waters of the Golden temple.

As many Sikhs took their holy dip, the occasional foreign tourist followed their lead, even drinking from the pool.

Location: Malang, Java, Indonesia.   **Date:** 25th April 2015

Riot police defend themselves on the streets of Malang.

Approaching the riot, camera in hand, it transpired that it was an exercise for Malang city's 101st year anniversary, with bags of water thrown at the often smiling police.

Location: Malang, Java, Indonesia.   **Date:** 25th April 2015

Women of the Indonesian army prepare for Malang's 101st year anniversary.

Full of fun, the women soldiers laughed in the streets of Malang, yet soon took a ferocious stance when called to duty.

Location: Bird Markets, Malang, Java, Indonesia.   **Date:** 25th April 2015

An Indonesian man sits beneath his collection of bird cages in the bird markets of Malang.

Amid the deafening sounds of bird call and screeching, the man sat peacefully with his prized birds.

Location: Boudhanath Stupa, Kathmandu, Nepal. **Date:** 12th September 2015

A Tibetan nun and her dog sit beside a shrine filled with candles on the steps of Boudha's stupa.

Found in the same place most days, the elderly nun gives blessings to devotees visiting the stupa.

Location: Sera Monastery, Lhasa, Tibet.   **Date:** 26th November 2014

Tibetan Buddhist monks debate in early evening on the courtyard of Sera monastery.

To the sounds of debate, laughter and the clapping of hands, security guards watched on, ready and eager to pounce on any tourist who stepped onto the white graveled courtyard, upon which this photograph was taken.

Location: Lamichhane Village, Sindhupalchowk, Nepal.　　　　**Date:** 21st April 2016

An earthquake affected family sit before their home high in the hills of Lamichhane village in the district of Sindhupalchowk surrounded by terraces of maize, barley and rice.

Working in conjunction with the Embassy of Finland, guided by the United Nations, the extended family told of the hardship they had experienced after the Nepal earthquakes of 2015.

Location: Boudhanath, Kathmandu, Nepal.   **Date:** 3rd October 2014

Afternoon sunlight plays through the window of the Buddhist temple of Boudhanath. Beside a large prayer wheel a Tibetan lady watches the world beyond the temple's walls.

Consistently busy with monks and nuns walking around the spinning wheel, the photo was taken in one shot before the room filled with devotees within seconds once more.

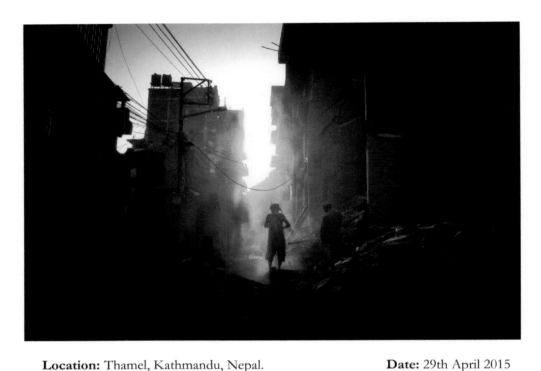

Location: Thamel, Kathmandu, Nepal.   **Date:** 29th April 2015

In rays of early evening sun on the dusty streets of Thamel, Kathmandu, Nepal, a family begins to clear the debris of where their former house stood before Nepal's earthquakes of April 25th and May 12th struck.

Stumbled upon on an evening walk around the block in the early evening, a series of eight shot were taken of the scene in the one minute when sun and dust combined.

Location: Thamel, Kathmandu, Nepal.   **Date:** 29th April 2016

A family sift through the rubble of their former home.

A stillness fell over the scene as the setting sun illuminated the dust strewn streets.

Location: Thamel, Kathmandu, Nepal.   **Date:** 19th March 2016

An elderly woman sits in the doorway of her shop in Kathmandu, Nepal.

In the Asian magic hour of 5pm to 6pm, warm sunlight caught the woman's features as she sat patiently waiting for customers in her vegetable shop.

Location: Thamel, Kathmandu, Nepal.   **Date:** 24th October 2014

An elderly Nepalese man outside his home in Thamel, Kathmandu.

Spending months passing by the man on the backstreets of Kathmandu, a brief raise of my camera to him produced a wonderful smile in return.

Location: Mai Sot, Western Thailand.   **Date:** 24th April 2005

The bound hands of Burmese boxer.

With no gloves allowed, the hemp wrapped hands of this Burmese Thai boxer made a formidable sight. He went on to win his weight category.

Location: Mai Sot, Western Thailand.   **Date:** 24th April 2005

Burmese and Thai boxers battle it out in their three round fight.

To relieve the tension between Burmese and Thai communities living in the area of the Burma/Thailand border town of Mai Sot, an annual three day boxing contest is held between close to one hundred Burmese and Thai boxers. As the day wore on alcohol fuelled crowds took delight in pulling photographers standing at the ropes of the ring.

Location: Mai Sot, Western Thailand.   **Date:** 24th April 2005

Seconds after the bell of the first round.

Not all contestants were natural fighters. The boxer lying on the floor fell down as soon as the first bell sounded, reluctant to fight, hence the referee's smiles and the other boxer's calls for his opponent to rise to his feet.

Location: The Burmese Border.   **Date:** 1st May 2005

A child soldier of the Karen National Liberation (K.N.L.A.) army   stands beside his RPG carrying uncle.

The dust and the heat of the K.N.L.A. training camp added no anxiety to the already dead pan stares of its boy soldiers.

Location: The Burmese Border.   **Date:** 1st May 2005

Child Soldiers of the K.N.L.A.

In the relentless Burmese afternoon sun, new recruits find solace in the shade, their guns as ever at their side.

Location: Oberoi Hotel, New Delhi, India.   **Date:** 4th January 2016

The Dalai Lama smiles at the Indian government's inauguration for His Holiness' 80th birthday at the Oberoi Hotel, New Delhi.

Having photographed His Holiness on three seperate occasions, a smile is always granted from Tibet's spiritual leader.

Location: The Golden Temple, Amritsar, Punjab, India.   **Date:** 6th January 2015

A Sikh devotee prays in the Golden temple of Amritsar.

As on all the watersides of the Golden temple's pool, devotees knelt down to pray before their sacred waters.

Location: The Golden Temple, Amritsar, Punjab, India.　　**Date:** 6th January 2015

Sikh of Amritsar.

A Sikh man dresses after immersing himself in the waters of the Golden temple's pool.

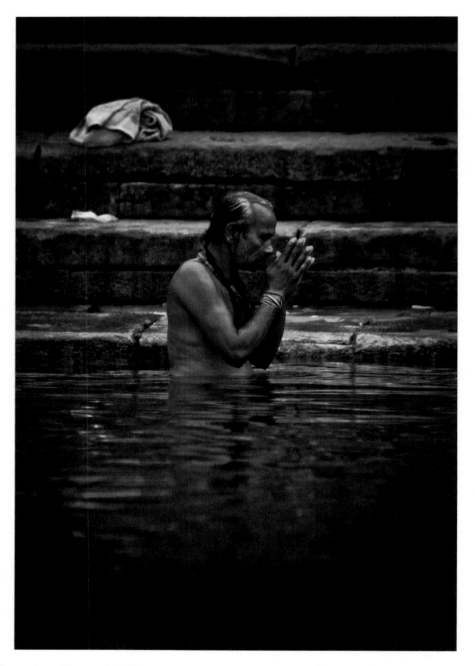

Location: Varanasi, India.   **Date:** 15th December 2014

A Hindu man prays in the river Ganges.

Millions of Hindu devotees visit Varanasi each year so they may wash away their sins in the Ganges' holy waters. The coloured tinge to the water is a result of ashes of the Ghats numerous funeral pyres being placed in the river.

Location: Varanasi, India.   **Date:** 15th December 2014

A man prepares himself to swim in the river ganges.

Photographs are forbidden along the Ghats. A boat trip along the waterside made for easy shooting, even though the calls and shouts from the river bank to stop led to being detained for a short while.

Location: The Dharavi Slums, Mumbai, India.　　　　　**Date:** 12th January 2015

Residents of the Dharavi slums of Mumbai.

With a population reaching nearly 1 million, the Dharavi slums of Mumbai are classed as the largest Asia. Founded during the British Empire in 1882, the Dharavi slum covers an area of over 500 acres. However, the slum has an active economy. Goods such as leather, textiles and pottery are made within by its inhabitants then exported around the world. It has been estimated that Dharavi's annual turnover is up to US$500 million.

When walking through a guided tour of the slums, one hour in the guide took into the heart of Dharavi, painting a very different picture to the outskirts of the slums which are primarily allocated to tourists.

Location: Phewa Lake, Pokhara, Nepal.   **Date:** 11th November 2014

On the waterfront of Phewa Lake in Nepal's second biggest city of Pokhara, a young woman sits leaning against a wall besides the small boats which ferry tourists across the lake.

Taking two shots, the first is the one shown above, the second shot a blur as the young woman pulled her sari across her features.

Location: Bhaktapur, Nepal.   **Date:** 11th May 2015

Mother and child outside their former home.

Just one of many buildings destroyed by the 25th April earthquake. Within less than 24 hours of taking this photograph a 7.3 magnitude earthquake would strike Nepal.

Location: Chhaimale Village, Nepal.   **Date:** 27th May 2015

Villagers of Chhaimale left homeless by Nepal's 2015 earthquakes.

Located 18Miles/29Km Southwest of Kathmandu, Chhaimale's residents congregated in the center of their village to receive donated solar lamps for their shelters.

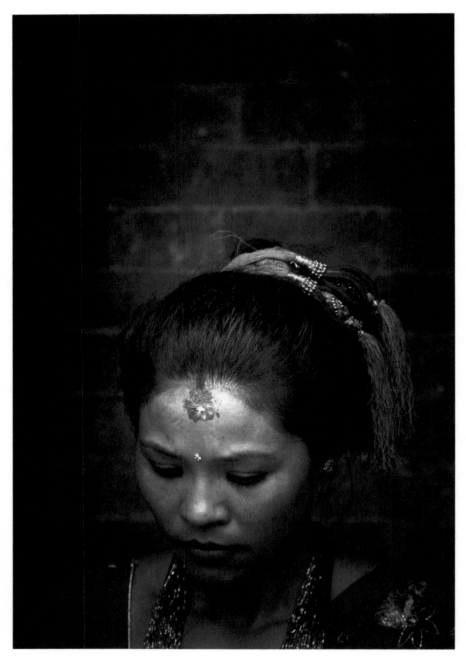

Location: Durbar Square, Kathmandu, Nepal.   **Date:** 16th September 2015

Teej festival is a celebration held by Nepali women for the long life of her husband and a long, firm relationship between them until their death in this lifetime or the next.

Although looking to be in quiet contemplation, she was playing with her phone, giving a big smile moments later to whatever had appeared across the screen.

Location: Kathmandu, Nepal.   **Date:** 7th October 2015

Lady selling slippers on the backstreets of Kathmandu.

Taken as the daylight hours gave way to night, the lady's bare feet added to the slippers surrounding her.

Location: Durbar Square, Kathmandu, Nepal.   **Date:** 7th October 2015

Nepalese man making drums.

Close to the entrance of Durbar square, the late evening sun highlighted the man and several of the drums made that day beside him.

Location: Mahadev Sthan Village, Sindhupalchowk, Nepal.   **Date:** 22nd April 2016

Woman of the village of Mahadev Sthan in the district of Sindhupalchowk.

Three days from the first anniversary of Nepal's 7.8 magnitude earthquake, the village of Mahadev Sthan still remains in deep recovery. With the majority of the village's two tiered homes destroyed, and after waiting for help from the government for close to one year, the villagers took into their own hands to start rebuilding that which was lost to them.

The parched red earth and barren landscape gave an eerie atmosphere to the village, marking the 35 lives lost there.

Location: Thamel, Kathmandu, Nepal.   **Date:** 5th November 2014

Rickshaw driver takes a break.

One of the many rickshaw drivers that navigate the chaotic traffic which belongs to Kathmandu takes a deserved break.

Taken in rush hour traffic, between the cars, motorbikes and other rickshaws, a gap appeared for a fraction of a second to capture the rickshaw driver's pensive moment.

Location: Ijen Volcano, East Java, Indonesia.　　　　　　**Date:** 29th April 2015

A sulpher miner takes a break half up Ijen volcano.

Taken wearing a cumbersome gas mask and with reddened eyes stinging from air thick with sulpher fumes, the miner seemed oblivious to the toxic atmosphere on resting next to the 90kg basket of raw sulpher beside him.

Location: Ijen Volcano, East Java, Indonesia.   **Date:** 29th April 2015

Inside the crater of the Ijen volcano in East Java, Indonesia, miners dig for sulpher, once known as brimstone, surrounded by noxious sulphur fumes.

The miners carry 90kg loads up a 800 meter steep, rocky path out of the crater and back down the volcano's outer slopes to a weighing station with little in the way of protective gear beyond a damp cloth to cover the nose and mouth.

Twice a day the miners collect these yellow lumps of sulphur that solidify beside its acidic crater lake. Once processed, the sulphur is used to bleach sugar, make matches and fertiliser, and to vulcanise rubber.

For one arduous trip a miner will receive on average $7 for their 90kg load.

Taken as the sun rose at 5:00am after starting out at 1am four hours earlier, the hardship of carrying camera equipment on the impossibly steep 3Km climb to the top of the volcano and then down an 800m rocky path in darkness paled in comparison to the two trips a day the miner above had made since fifteen years old.

Location: Lakeside, Pokhara, Nepal.   **Date:** 16th November 2014

Farmers take a break in their fields beside Pokhara's Phewa Lake.

On the last day of harvest, the farmers sat together for lunch. Inviting their new guest to join them, the language barrier disappeared as we enjoyed lava hot chai in equally hot metal cups.

In the background can be seen other farmers carry their crops over their body

Location: Lakeside, Pokhara, Nepal.   **Date:** 16th November 2014

Villager's carry their crops.

From the fields surrounding Phewa lake, the best way for the farmers to carry their produce to the awaiting roadside is the centuries old technique displayed above.

Location: Chhaimale Village, Nepal.   **Date:** 27th May 2015

Woman of Chhaimale village.

Documenting solar lanterns being distributed by Nepal and a UK based NGOs in the village of Chhaimale, all afternoon the woman pictured would not allow for her photo to be taken. As we were about to leaving the village, she gave me a smile and this single opportunity.

Location: Jethal, Sindhupalchowk, Nepal.   **Date:** 15th October 2015

Woman of Jethal village in the district of Sindhupalchowk, Nepal.

After a day documenting the work of Nepalese NGO 'Himalayan Aid' throughout the Sindhupalchowk district and high up on the Tibetan borders, the woman's wind seared cheeks added to the red walls and blanket as she sat opposite me in a small tea shop.

Location: Durbar Square, Kathmandu, Nepal.   **Date:** 25th April 2016

Woman in doorway.

In the early evening light, a women sits in the doorway of her home on the street leading from Thamel to Durbar square. Walking these streets often, the real Nepal can be seen, where laughter, car horns and music fill the air already filled with life.

Location: Jethal, Sindhupalchowk, Nepal. **Date:** 15th October 2015

Woman of Jethal village in the district of Sindhupalchowk.

An elderly villager watches all that is going on around her community.

Location: Jethal, Sindhupalchowk, Nepal.   **Date:** 15th October 2015

Woman of Jethal village.

Just miles from the Tibetan border with Nepal, the sharp cold of approaching winter encouraged the community to wrap up in blankets of yak hair.

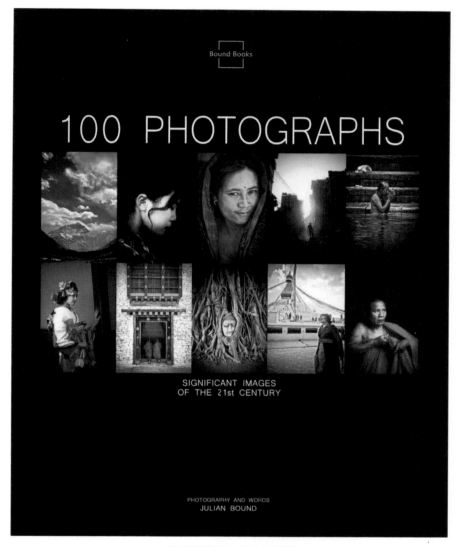

100 PHOTOGRAPHS

A collection of 100 photographs from
Nepal, Tibet, Japan, India, Bhutan, Thailand, Cambodia, Laos, Indonesia, Myanmar and England.

With images from eleven countries by documentary photographer Julian Bound, '100 Photographs' is a representation of how the world is now, and how the emotional characteristics of the human condition remains unswerving throughout the changes surrounding it.

These emotive aspects are portrayed within 100 unique photographic views of the world, revealed in the happiness of novice monks at play in the high walled fortress monasteries of Bhutan, the pensive stares of street vendors on the cobblestone lanes of the Nepalese capital Kathmandu, and the determination of sulphur miners earning a living amid the hazardous conditions of Indonesia's active volcanoes.

In Print and E-Book Format at AMAZON.COM

CONFLICT
DISASTER RELIEF
SOCIAL COMMENTARY
EMERGENCY DEPLOYMENT

PHOTOGRAPHY AND WORDS
JULIAN BOUND

HOW TO BE A DOCUMENTARY PHOTOGRAPHER

Set within the locations of Myanmar, Nepal, Thailand, Indonesia and India, a photographic insight into the aspects of conflict photography, social commentary, emergency disaster deployment and disaster relief.

A definitive guide for anyone considering a career in documentary photography.

Available to buy in Print or E-Book at Amazon.com

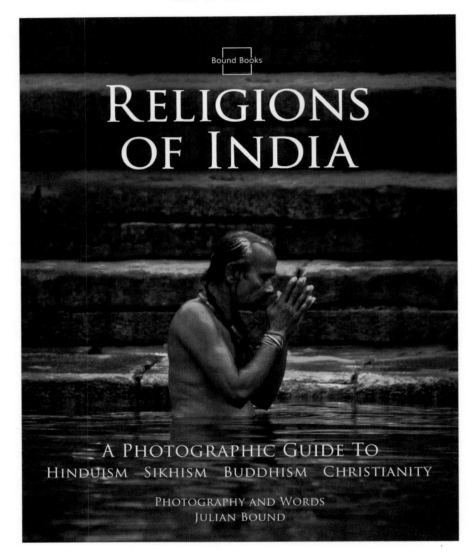

RELIGIONS OF INDIA

A photographic account of Hinduism, Sikhism, Buddhism and Christianity throughout India.

From Hindu's bathing in Varanasi's mighty Ghats on the banks of the sacred River Ganges, Brahmin priests of southern India, and Sikhs worshiping in Amritsar's 'Golden Temple', to Buddhism, and His Holiness the 14th Dalai Lama in his home of McLeod Ganj, Dharamsala, and the Buddhist devotees on their pilgrimage to Bodh Gaya and its famed Bodhi tree, to the Portuguese legacy of Catholicism, still thriving today amid ornate churches and chapels on the beaches and cliff tops of India's western state of Goa.

A beautiful representation of India's religious beliefs
with over 100 photographs in colour and black and white.

Available for download at Amazon.com

TIBET

A photographic journey through Tibet's villages, landscapes, towns and the capital city of Lhasa by award winning documentary photographer Julian Bound.

From the Tibetan Everest base camp to the world's highest mountain pass of Ganchula and the 14,570feet/4,441m high Yamdrok Lake, passing through the snow capped peaks of the Himalaya and onwards to the monasteries and temples of Drepung and Sera of Lhasa, and Jokhang Temple in the heart of the Tibetan capital. With over 100 photographs in colour and black and white.

Available for download at Amazon.com

Bound Books

TIBETAN

TIBET

NEPAL

INDIA

A PORTRAIT OF THE TIBETAN PEOPLE

JULIAN BOUND

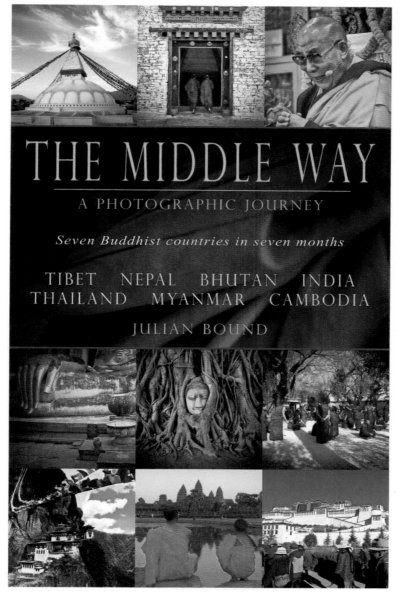

THE MIDDLE WAY

Documenting Buddhism in India, Nepal, Bhutan, Tibet, Myanmar, Thailand and Cambodia, a 6,331mile/10,156km photographic journey through seven Buddhist countries in seven months by award winning documentary photographer Julian Bound.

From McLeod Ganj, India's 'Little Lhasa', to the secluded fortresses of Bhutan, Tibet's high altitude monasteries, Myanmar and Thailand's golden temples and Cambodia's riverside shrines.

Travelling through altitudes of 16,900 feet/5,150 meters to sea level, and temperatures between -18 to 38 degrees, a journey of discovery on the path of the middle way.

Available for download at Amazon.com

PHOTOGRAPHY BOOKS

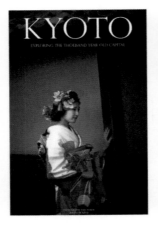

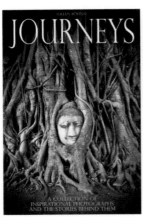

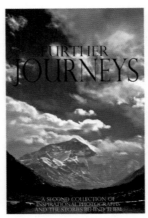

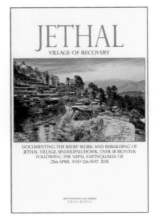

DOCUMENTING ASIA
VOLUMES 1 - 9

THE GEISHA AND THE MONK

Two souls born thousands of miles apart.
Together each shall follow a similar path.

Japan, 1876
A girl is born, her life path to become the famed Geisha she is destined to be.

Tibet, 1876
A boy is born, ordained to be the revered Lama he is recognised as.

San Francisco, 1900
At the dawning of a new century fate brings them together,
a lifetime away from all they have ever known.

The Geisha and The Monk is a story of love and compassion, holding many answers to life's questions which are explained through Buddhist teachings.
As well as sharing an insight into the preparation and life of a Geisha, The Geisha and The Monk explores the seldom known life and training of a Buddhist monk within Tibet's monasteries.

Available in paperback and E-book download at Amazon.com

ALSO BY THE AUTHOR

FICTION

LIFE'S HEART ETERNAL

One man's journey through the centuries

'My name is Franc Barbour. I was born on the 20th July 1845 in the town of Saumur, deep in the heart of the Loire Valley, France. The truth of the matter is I simply never died.'

These are the opening words a young nurse reads in an old leather bound journal given to her by a stranger. She soon uncovers the story of one man's journey through the centuries. Following Franc's path from 1845 until present day, 'Life's Heart Eternal' is a tale of how our actions in each lifetime hold consequences in the next.

With Franc's travels across the world in his endless years, the reader anticipates his next encounter with those reincarnated from his past and of what lessons each shall meet with.

'For who has never wondered what it would be like to live forever?'

SUBWAY OF LIGHT

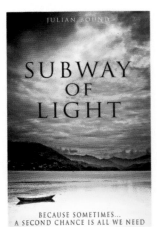

A heart warming modern day tale of kindness and understanding.

Following an accident, Josh finds himself sat alone at the back of an empty New York subway car on a deserted station, his memory gone and with no recollection of how he arrived there. A man approaches and introduces himself as George. He tells Josh he has been taken out of his life to partake on a journey on the train. Acting as a guide, George explains their train will make several stops and that each station they visit may begin to seem familiar to him.

Arriving at their first stop, they witness a young couple meet for the first time. George tells Josh the young couple are soulmates rediscovering one another again. At the ensuing subway stations they follow the young couple's life as they experience courtship, marriage, tragedy and happiness. Watching their lives unfold Josh's memory starts to return, until he himself must decide the fate of his own final destination.

THE SOUL WITHIN

In releasing our thoughts towards a lifetime imagined,
only then may we have the life our soul awaits.

Falling ill in his home town of Puri on India's eastern coastline, a boy is visited by his spirit guide. Taking him on a journey around a tranquil lake, together they observe those living along its banks.

As his guide explains the life lessons they encounter through her subtle teachings, the boy's emerging awareness to matters of the soul leads him to discover the reasons behind their meeting as his story unfolds.

Because everyone longs for
their soul to be touched

Available in paperback and E-book download at Amazon.com

THE SEVEN DEADLY SINS AND THE SEVEN HEAVENLY

Perceived as being associated within the doctrine of the Christian faith, the eastern religions of Buddhism, Hinduism and Sikhism all share a parallel view of the seven sins and virtues, yet are expressed in the theology of different precepts.

'The Seven Deadly Sins and The Seven Heavenly Virtues' examines the similarities of each sin and virtue within religions of the world, and of the portrayal in mythology and art and literature.

'The Seven Deadly Sins and The Seven Heavenly Virtues' also invites the reader to identify which sin they are prone to and of what virtue best displays their greatest qualities; the result of which is an exploration of the self within the aspects of the seven sins and seven virtues, and so acting as a guide for each soul's unique individual path.

Available in paperback and E-book download at Amazon.com

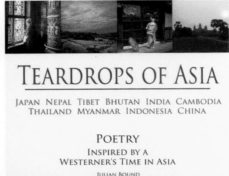

HAIKU, A JOURNEY THROUGH THE DEEPEST EMOTIONS

Using the traditional Japanese form of haiku poetry to evoke a thought or emotion within its unique simplicity of creation. Following the four key elements of self, each poem is presented to the reader for contemplation and meditation on both the physical and metaphysical world around them.

ON NATURE
The foundations of all life itself.
ON MIND
The primary strides towards awareness of being.
ON LOVE
The practice of awareness, the deepness of the self.
ON BEING
The act of living a life filled with and emitting love.
ON CALMNESS
The tranquillity of finding stillness of mind and being.

TEARDROPS OF ASIA

An anthology of Japanese Haiku and traditional poetry influenced by a nine year journey through Asia and South East Asia by award winning documentary photographer Julian Bound.

Drawing on the sights, sounds and emotions of a continent filled with such rich diversity of life, traditions and cultures, 'Teardrops of Asia' examines the unified depths of the differing qualities of each country, from the tranquill Japanese gardens of Kyoto, to the barren landscapes of southern Tibet, the riverside temples of northern Cambodia and the remote monastery fortresses of central Bhutan.

Available in paperback and E-book download at Amazon.com

THIS NOBLE HUNT

A collection of poetry inspired by situations encountered during a twenty year career as a documentary photographer. From the documenting of the boy soldiers of the Burmese Karen National Liberation Army, to the Arab Spring of 2011, Cairo, Egypt, to the gypsies of India and resettled Tibetan refugees in Nepal, each poetic chapter offers an insight into the emotions present within such times.

From award winning documentary photographer Julian Bound, 'This Noble Hunt' also explores the assignments of the sulphur miners of Java, the Nepalese earthquakes of 2015 and His Holiness the 14th Dalai Lama's 80th birthday. From the bestselling author of 'The Geisha and the Monk' and 'How to be a Documentary Photographer'.

A CURIOUS JOURNEY

A collection of poetry inspired by a lifetime of travel from award winning documentary photographer Julian Bound.

From a first venture of travel to Paris, then onwards to the Pacific islands of Fiji and The Cook Islands, to the sights of Asian delight and to the exploring of mysticism in the foothills of the Tibetan Himalaya, each encounter and location is portrayed with great heart in the sentiments discovered both of mind and of soul on this curious of journeys to all four corners of the world.

Available in paperback and E-book download at Amazon.com

The author sits with Gen Lama, one of the Gyuto monks who escaped Tibet at His Holiness the 14th Dalai Lama's side on 17th March 1959.

The Gyuto Tantric Monastery, Sidhbari, Dharamsala, India.
13th February 2016

IN THE FIELD

Earthquake relief, Baadbhanjang Village,
Nepal, 2015

The Karmapa Temple, Gyuto Tantric Monastery,
Dharamsala, India, 2016

Earthquake shelters, Chhaimale Village,
Nepal, 2015

KNLA Army Camp
Myanmar, 2004

Earthquake relief, Jethal Village, Sindhupalchowk, Nepal, 2015

Printed in Great Britain
by Amazon